People Who Help Us

The Police

Clare Oliver

Photographs: Chris Fairclough

FRANKLIN WATTS

LONDON • SYDNEY

This edition 2007

First published in 2002 by
Franklin Watts
338 Euston Road
London
NW1 3BH

Franklin Watts Australia
Level 17/207 Kent Street
Sydney
NSW 2000

A CIP catalogue record for this book is available
from the British Library.

ISBN 978 0 7496 7272 0
Dewey Decimal Classification Number 363.2

Series Editor: Jackie Hamley
Cover Design: Peter Scoulding
Design: Sally Boothroyd

Photos
All commissioned photographs by Chris Fairclough.
The publishers would like to thank the following for permission to use photographs:
www.shoutpictures.com 22, 23, 24; Ian Kenins/Sporting Pictures (UK) Ltd 26;
AP Photo/US Drug Enforcement/Gamma/Frank Spooner Pictures 27

Every attempt has been made to clear copyright. Should there be any
inadvertent omission, please apply to the publisher for recification.

The author and publisher would especially like to thank members of
Wimbledon police station for giving their help and time so generously.

Note to parents and teachers: Every effort has been made by the Publishers to ensure that the websites
in this book are suitable for children; that they are of the highest educational value, and that they
contain no inappropriate or offensive material. However, because of the nature of the Internet, it is
impossible to guarantee that the contents of these sites will not be altered. We strongly advise that
Internet access is supervised by a responsible adult.

Printed in Malaysia

Franklin Watts is a division of Hachette Children's Books.

Contents

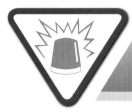

Meet the team

▦ Every day, the police help people in all sorts of ways.

Most police stations are open around the clock. The police work in **shifts**, so there are always people on duty to help us.

In this book, you will meet police officers and other staff from Wimbledon police station. They are part of the Metropolitan Police Service, the police force that looks after most of London.

Here are some of the team from Wimbledon police station.

1 Paula **2** Shelley **3** Bob **4** Colin **5** John
6 James **7** Kevin **8** Dave **9** Stuart **10** Pete
11 Belle **12** Lucy **13** Graham **14** Obi **15** Adam

There are many different sections in the police force. They include **detectives**, **mounted** police, traffic police and many more. There are also **volunteers** who help the police. All the different sections work together to keep us safe.

Many police officers wear uniforms to do their jobs. They also carry lots of useful equipment.

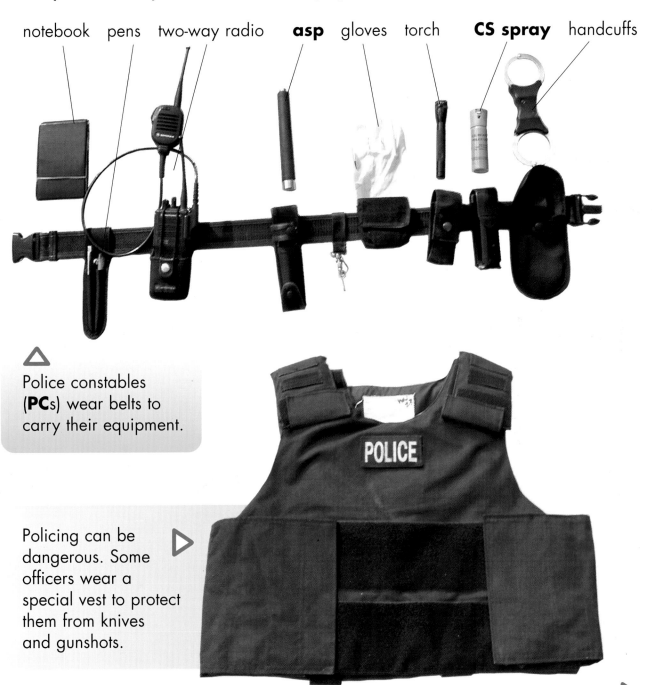

notebook   pens   two-way radio   **asp**   gloves   torch   **CS spray**   handcuffs

▲ Police constables (**PC**s) wear belts to carry their equipment.

▷ Policing can be dangerous. Some officers wear a special vest to protect them from knives and gunshots.

POLICE

Dealing with crime

▦ The main way that the police help people is by preventing and solving crimes.

Crimes are actions that break the law, such as stealing or hurting another person. The police solve crimes, find **criminals** and help **victims**.

Burglary is a crime. This house-owner shows police constable (PC) Kevin where the burglars broke in through the window.

The police also try to stop crime happening in the future. For example, they work with parents, teachers and other people to help children understand the law.

The police do other things to help us in the local community. They give advice about how to stay safe and keep your house secure. They help people find their way around the area, too.

PC Kevin gives directions to a mother who is visiting the town.

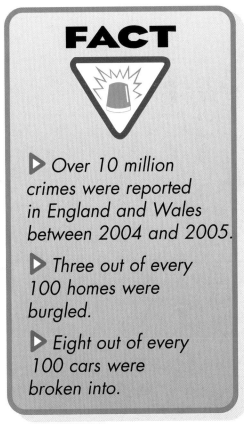

FACT

▷ Over 10 million crimes were reported in England and Wales between 2004 and 2005.

▷ Three out of every 100 homes were burgled.

▷ Eight out of every 100 cars were broken into.

The police know about crimes because people report them.

People report crimes over the phone, or in person at the police station. They also visit the station to hand in lost property, such as purses, keys or even dogs!

Shelley is not a police officer. She works on the front desk of the police station where she meets people who come in.

A woman hands in a purse she has found. Perhaps the person who lost it has already reported it missing.

But when people need urgent police help, they dial the emergency number. The call goes to the nearest police station's control room. The officers who work there are in radio contact with everyone on duty. They send police officers to respond to emergency calls.

The control-room officers use their computers to check on **suspects**, and watch the streets using **CCTV** (Closed Circuit Television).

FACT

▷ CCTV cameras film inside shops and out on our streets. They allow police and security guards to watch for trouble in a lot of places at the same time.

▷ There are 25 million CCTV cameras in the world today; 2.5 million of them are in the UK.

▷ In the UK, people are seen on CCTV cameras on average 300 times every day.

Can you see the CCTV screens? Steve can watch the town centre while he takes emergency calls.

PC Kevin receives information from the control room on his radio.

On the beat

PCs (police constables) look after particular areas, or beats.

When PCs are on the **beat**, it means they are patrolling their own area on foot or by bicycle.

PCs on the beat must always be ready for action. They have to respond to emergency radio calls from the control room. They also watch out for street fights, robberies and other crimes.

▲ PC Kevin uses a bicycle on his beat.

PCs Dave and Lucy wear bright coats when they are on the beat. This makes them easy to spot for anyone who needs their help.

Sometimes, PCs radio for help. They may need a patrol car to take a suspect back to the police station after an **arrest**, or help in finding a suspect.

At the police station, and out on patrol, there are officers in cars ready to come and help officers on the beat. This help is called "back-up".

▷ PCs write down what they do, see and hear. Their notebooks may be used as **evidence** in **court**.

Back-up request granted! The letters and numbers on a patrol car's roof help the police helicopters identify it. ▷

In for questioning

■ **A person suspected of breaking the law is arrested and taken to the police station.**

At the police station, the suspect meets the **custody officer**. The custody officer is always a **sergeant**. He or she asks the suspect some questions and writes down the information on a form.

PC Lucy has arrested a suspect. Paul is the custody officer. He asks for the suspect's name, age, address and other details.

Roger scans the suspect's fingerprints. The machine is linked straight to Scotland Yard, the headquarters of the Metropolitan Police. All the fingerprints from criminals across the UK are kept on record here.

PC Kevin takes a mouth swab to sample the suspect's **DNA**.

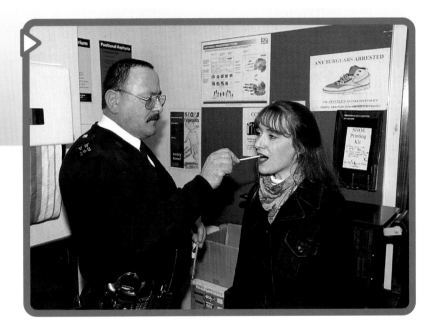

The suspect is kept in the police station's **cells**. Young people are kept in separate detention rooms.

The form goes into the police records. The police also take fingerprints, a photograph and, sometimes, a DNA sample. DNA is the special code of life that makes each person different.

Next, the suspect is locked up in the cells. Later, he or she will be questioned about the crime.

FACT

▷ Every person has a unique set of fingerprints – no two people have the same.

▷ At the scene of a crime, officers use a special powder that shows up any fingerprints left by the criminals.

▷ If the police suspect somebody of doing the crime, they can compare their fingerprints with any fingerprints left at the crime scene.

Detectives

Detectives look for clues and collect evidence to try and solve crimes.

Detectives are police officers who are part of the Criminal Investigation Department (CID). They do not wear uniform. Sometimes they work **undercover** to find out information.

CID detectives work with other police officers to do their job.

If detectives suspect someone of a crime, they look for evidence to see whether or not the person is **guilty**.

PC Kevin briefs Colin, the CID detective who will be taking over the **case**.

> *Questioning suspects or witnesses is quite difficult. You have to persuade them to talk and give you information – even if they don't want to.*
> **Colin, CID officer**

Colin questions the suspect in the interview room.

When a suspect is questioned, it is called an interview. Interviews are always recorded on a tape. Sometimes the tape is used as evidence.

If the officers think the suspect is guilty and they have evidence to prove it, they take the case to a court of law.

Ibrahim is a detective. Today, he is giving evidence in court.

Helping paws

▪ Dogs are very useful members of the police force.

A police dog goes to live with its handler when it is still a puppy. The pair will work as a team for many years, so it is important that they are good friends.

Graham and Obi have worked together for five years.

In this training exercise, Obi has followed the scent to a suspect. He barks to alert Graham.

Dogs have a very good sense of smell. They can sniff out clues or drugs, track down burglars or help find missing people.

Dogs are trained to grip suspects on the right arm. Handlers wear a bite-proof sleeve!

Traffic police

So many accidents happen on the roads that there is a special section of traffic police.

This driver was going too fast. He blows into the breathalyser.

Traffic police patrol in cars or on motorbikes. They go to traffic accidents and they also stop anyone who is driving dangerously.

When drivers are stopped by the police, they may have to blow into a **breathalyser**. This machine tests the driver's breath and shows if he or she has been drinking alcohol.

Drink-driving is a serious crime and can cause very bad traffic accidents.

Andy is part of the traffic police. His bike has a computer, so he can receive information about accidents and other emergencies. He also carries a first aid kit.

Andy reads information from the computer on his dashboard.

FACT

▷ All motorbike traffic officers must pass an advanced motorbike driving course before going out on the road.

▷ Some police vehicles are kept in the police yard – ready for any trained officer to drive in an emergency.

Police traffic wardens are part of the police force, too. They make sure that vehicles are parked safely.

They also check that vehicles on the road are safe to drive, and whether they have an up-to-date **road tax** disc.

Police traffic wardens check the road tax disc on this vehicle.

All kinds of transport

Bikes, cars and vans are not the only vehicles the police have to get around.

The police use lots of different kinds of transport. Horses are used to control crowds – at marches or carnivals, for example.

Mounted police get a good view to help them control the crowds.

Boats carry police divers searching for missing people or evidence. They are also used to catch criminals.

Helicopters help patrol cars on the ground during a chase. They even have special **infra-red cameras** so they can see in the dark.

> *The last time I worked with the helicopter team was when someone had escaped from the nearby prison. We found the man really quickly – before he had a chance to put anyone in danger.*
> **Dave, PC**

A police diver hands a metal bar he has found to another officer. This might be evidence.

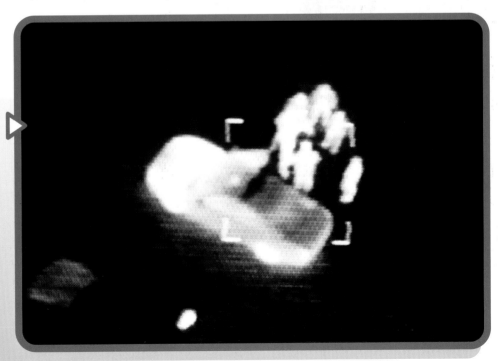

An infra-red camera in a helicopter shows a gang of burglars with the car they used in a robbery. The helicopter crew will pass information to officers on the ground.

Joining forces

■ Sometimes the police team up with other people who help us.

The police work closely with ambulance crews and firefighters. This often happens at traffic accidents.

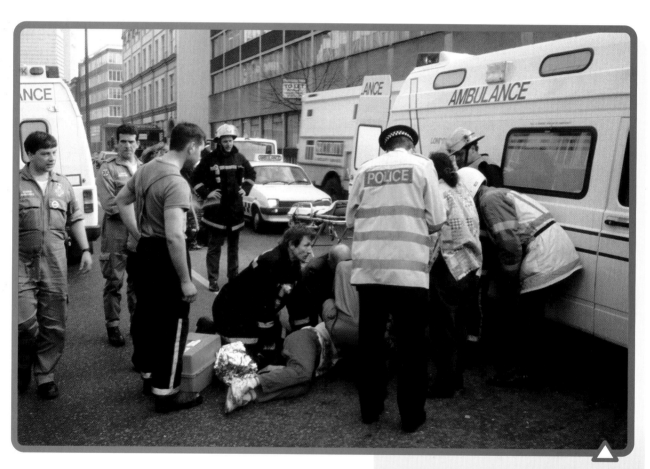

The police work side by side with ambulance crews and firefighters to help someone who has been hit by a car.

The police also work with Victim Support, a group that helps victims of crime. And the police help local people prevent crime, through Neighbourhood Watch and other schemes.

The police also try to help criminals stop committing crimes. If a criminal has a drug problem, for example, he or she can talk to someone in the police station about it and get help. This may be the criminal's first step towards a future without crime.

The National Neighbourhood Watch Association is a charity that helps local people work with the police to protect their communities.
To find out more, see page 30.

Mark listens to people who are under arrest. He talks to them **in confidence** and tries to help them cope with drug and other problems.

> **Without help from the public, solving crimes would be almost impossible. We rely on people telling us what they know – and they can give information in confidence.**
> **Colin, CID detective**

Help in action

Many crimes are the same around the world, and the police forces in different countries work hard to deal with them.

Police forces work in different ways. But they all try to make our communities more secure by preventing and solving crimes. Just by being there, they can make events safer and more enjoyable for everyone.

An Australian police officer looks after the crowd at Melbourne Cricket Ground.

A drug smuggler from Colombia is arrested by police in America.

At times, police forces from different countries work together. This might happen because a criminal left the country where the crime happened and went to another country.

Crimes can take place across several countries. To solve them, different police forces work together. International crimes include terrorism and drug smuggling.

Interpol is an organisation that was set up over 75 years ago. It helps police around the world catch criminals by sharing information. At the moment, 179 countries are Interpol members.

Keeping safe

- Make sure that a grown-up you know – your parent or a teacher – knows where you are.

- Never talk to strangers or go off with someone you don't know. If a stranger approaches you, tell a grown-up you know.

- If you see a crime, you can help the police by telling them what you have seen. Don't try to stop the crime yourself.

- Don't join in if other people are breaking the law. Laws are there to keep everyone safe.

- Always be careful!

DIALLING 999

Dial 000 in Australia.

Only ever dial 999 in a real emergency. It is against the law to make a **hoax** call and it could put someone else's life in danger. Be ready to:

1. Ask for the emergency service you need, for example "Police".

2. Say exactly where the police are needed.

3. Say exactly what the trouble is.

4. Give your name and the number of the telephone you're calling from.

5. Stay on the line until the control-room officer says you can hang up.

Don't worry about answering lots of questions. While you are talking, the police will already be on their way.

Glossary

arrest Police arrest people if they think they have broken the law.

asp An extending baton.

beat The area that a police officer patrols and is responsible for.

breathalyser A device that shows how much alcohol is in the body.

case A crime that the police are trying to solve.

CCTV (Closed Circuit Television) A video camera that records what is happening in a particular place.

cell A small room where people are held and cannot get out of.

court The place where matters of law are decided.

criminal A person who commits a crime.

CS spray A spray that makes people unable to see or breathe properly for a while.

custody officer The person who looks after people in police cells or under arrest.

detectives Police officers who investigate serious crimes.

DNA The special code inside your body that only you have and that makes you unique.

evidence Something that will prove that a fact is true.

guilty If someone is guilty, it means he or she did the crime.

hoax Fake or joke.

in confidence Secretly.

infra-red cameras Special equipment that shows heat, so the police can see in the dark.

mounted On horseback.

PC (police constable) A police officer – this is the rank at which police enter the police force.

road tax A tax that must be paid on a vehicle to allow it on the road.

sergeant A police officer who is a rank above a constable.

shifts Periods of work planned so someone is on duty at all times.

suspect A person who is thought to have broken the law.

undercover Secretly working without saying who you really are.

victim A person who has been hurt by someone or something.

volunteer Someone who offers his or her time for free.

witness Someone who has seen a crime or accident.

Further information

It takes 18 weeks of training to become a police officer, followed by two years of further training at a police station. There are also many other jobs in the police force, for which you do not need to train as an officer.

To find out more about the Metropolitan Police, visit:
www.met.police.uk

To find out more about Neighbourhood Watch, visit:
www.neighbourhoodwatch.net
Or visit your local police station.

To find out more about the police in Australia, visit:
www.afp.gov.au
This is a website for the Federal Police, but it also has links to the local police force websites.

Index